Cow Pie Ain't No Dish You Take to the County Fair

AND OTHER COWBOY FACTS OF LIFE

WITH ILLUSTRATIONS
BY JIM WILLOUGHBY

ARIZONA
HIGHWAYS

Cow Pie Ain't No Dish You Take to the County Fair And Other Cowboy Facts of Life was written by 15 *Arizona Highways* contributors. They are:

PRINCIPAL AUTHOR
Ida Ewing

OTHER AUTHORS

Cindy Essendrup	Scott Parrish
Kim Essendrup	Barbara Anne Pease
Paul Heller	Jeb Stuart Rosebrook
Mary C. Hughes	Judith A. Schroedl
Christine Maxa	Paula Searcy
Carrie Miner	Debbie Stack
Sara W. O'Neal	Jill Welch

The cowboy illustrations and the 'reviews' on the back cover come from the creative mind of Jim Willoughby of Prescott.

The cartoons of Willoughby, who for years created storyboards for Hollywood's top animation studios, have appeared in hundreds of magazines, including *Look, Saturday Evening Post, Colliers,* and *Family Circle.*

Considered among the West's greatest cowboy cartoonists, Willoughby's work appears regularly in *Arizona Highways.*

DEDICATED
to all those courageous adults
who undergo untold sacrifices
to return to colleges and universities
in an effort to expand their learning
and improve their lives.

Prepared by the Book Division of *Arizona Highways*® magazine, a monthly publication of the Arizona Department of Transportation.

PUBLISHER: NINA M. LA FRANCE   MANAGING EDITOR: BOB ALBANO
ASSOCIATE EDITOR: ROBERT J. FARRELL   ART DIRECTOR: MARY WINKELMAN VELGOS
PRODUCTION DIRECTOR: CINDY MACKEY

**"HEY, COOKIE,
WHAT'S IN THIS STEW?"**

CONTENTS

**"I WISH HE'D LOOK AT ME
THAT WAY."**

COWBOY
WISDOM

Some call it headstrong,
some say independent,
but cowboys call it
a way of life.

Never cheat
at poker or women.
They'll both leave you
broke, lonely,
and sometimes
with a bullet
in the belly.

In the pasture,
you won't find
all-beef patties
with special sauce,
lettuce, or cheese,
but they do come
with chips.

Bad whiskey,
like bad advice,
should be taken lightly.

Never play leapfrog
with a longhorn.

Show me a
saddlesore cowboy,
and I'll show you one
with a raw hide.

If English saddles
don't have horns,
how do English riders
let you know they want to pass?

Fishermen talk
about the fish
that got away,
and cowboys talk about
the cows that didn't.

A cowboy who forgoes
his Saturday night bath
is unlikely
to spur the attention
of the schoolmarm
on Sunday morning,
and will likely
have to sit in
his own "pew."

Today a cowboy's
faithful companion
is most often his pickup truck.

Spurs
are to cowboys
what crowns
are to kings.

What do you call a cowboy
who puts salt on his beans?
A gourmet.

A horse in the corral
is worth 20 on the range.

Don't leave it
to the marshal
to look out
for your best interest.

A cowboy
in the kitchen
is seldom
at home
on the range.

Bridle:
A device used
to control a horse.

Bridal:
A device used
to control a cowboy.

Both are just fancy trappings
meant to control
a feisty steed.

Know
what you want to rope
before
you throw the lasso.

If you can't find your way home
and it's close to dinnertime,
trust your horse.

Bronc-bustin' and weddings
accomplish the same thing.

Time is like a cowboy,
always packing up
and moving away.

Don't swap horses
in the middle
of a raging river.

You can fool
all of the horses
some of the time,
and some of the horses
all of the time,
but you can never
fool Trigger.

The saguaro said to the cholla,
"You see those two
unshaven cowboys?
Now that's a prickly pair."

Too bad you can't cross
a horse and a cow.
That way you could
ride the critter to market.

Cowboys are weather-wise;
city folks are otherwise.

A good woman
is like a good hat.
She holds tight
but doesn't
mess up your head.

Sows, don't let your piglets
grow up to be footballs.

Cowboys
smoke their meat
and chew
their tobacco.

You can tell a happy cowboy
by the bugs on his teeth.

An old-timer remembers
when a burro was a wild donkey
and not a Mexican snack.

Cowboys have three speeds:
mosey, lope, and
"the bull's out of the pen!"

One step at a time
keeps a cowboy
from having to clean
his boots.

If the best
a cowboy can do
is display
a marvelous grasp
of the obvious,
don't bother.

A rolling stone
gathers no moss,
but it settles coffee grounds
just fine.

The worse
you are shot,
the faster your horse
needs to be.

Urban cowboys
have horseshoes made by Gucci.

You know a cowboy's
interested in a woman
when he comments
on how pretty
her teeth are.

Never sit close to the campfire
when eating beans.

Cowboys always
learn the ropes.

A cowboy
who gets his leathers wet
will soon have his
chaps stick.

Even when
hope and science fail us,
cowboy art survives.

Real cowboys might not die,
but they sometimes
smell like they did.

A cowboy can keep
a steer tied up
with a good rope,
but a good woman
can keep a cowboy tied up
with just a smile.

"WOW, HOW SWEET, RIMSHOT!
AN ALFALFA BOUQUET!"

"I DON'T THINK THE COWS
WILL EVEN NOTICE, PITCHFORK."

REAL COWBOYS

YOU'RE A REAL COWBOY IF YOU:

Know where
Rocky Mountain oysters come from
and eat them anyway.

Think a wok
is a good way to exercise.

YOU'RE A REAL COWBOY IF YOU:

Believe
gene-splicing
is ripping
your Wranglers.

Think gene therapy means
mending your Wranglers.

YOU'RE A REAL COWBOY IF YOU:

Believe a hacker
is a guy who cuts wood.

Think a mobile phone
is one that's not
nailed to the wall.

YOU'RE A REAL COWBOY IF YOU:

Have a horse, a dog, and
a pickup truck
as your best friends.

Would rather face outlaws
than in-laws.

YOU'RE A REAL COWBOY IF YOU:

Believe a
home page is
the real-estate
section of the local paper.

Think a floppy disc
is a weak back.

YOU'RE A REAL COWBOY IF YOU:

Think fuel injection
means tossing another
log on the fire.

Can hit a target
at 200 yards
and a spittoon at 10 feet.

YOU'RE A REAL COWBOY IF YOU:

Believe a Cuisinart is one of those modern paintings that make you sick just looking at them.

Use alfalfa for horse feed and not for salad garnish.

YOU'RE A REAL COWBOY IF YOU:

Believe networking is an illegal but effective way to catch trout.

Think a web site is a spider's home.

YOU'RE A REAL COWBOY IF YOU:

Think downloading means
getting the cows off the truck . . .

and uploading means
putting them back on.

YOU'RE A REAL COWBOY IF YOU:

Think an organ transplant means moving a pipe organ from one church to another.

YOU'RE A REAL COWBOY IF YOU:

Think a computer-aided draft
ended with the war in Vietnam.

Use the name on your belt buckle
as a form of ID.

YOU'RE A REAL COWBOY IF YOU:

Think dual exhaust means
getting plumb tuckered out
from facing down
two bad guys at high noon.

YOU'RE A REAL COWBOY IF YOU:

Consider Wranglers
your basic wardrobe.

Feel naked outdoors without a hat.

YOU'RE A REAL COWBOY IF YOU:

Think a bola tie and clean jeans
qualify as formal wear.

Wear boots with a tux.

YOU'RE A REAL COWBOY IF YOU:

Believe a laptop
is a fitting place
to deposit pretty girls
and bowls of stew.

Think animal research means
looking for the lost cows — again.

"IT JUST AIN'T 'COWBOY,' BUCKSHOT."

"WHAT COLOR
IS YOUR HORSE, COWBOY?"

"WHO HIRED THIS GUY?"

"DON'T TELL ME.
THEY CALL YOU 'SLIM,' RIGHT?"

A FEW GOOD RIDDLES

Why did the cowboy
sing soprano?

BECAUSE HE HAD A BIG RANGE.

Why did the cowboy tie a pistol to his bronc?

BECAUSE HE WANTED MORE BANG FOR HIS BUCK.

How did the lynching party make the outlaw take a chance?

THEY PUT HIM OUT ON A LIMB.

Why did Lassie cry when she ate the cantaloupe?

BECAUSE SHE WAS MELON-COLLIE.

Why did the cowboy's boss
take him to the Western store?

BOOTS

BECAUSE HE WANTED TO GIVE HIM
THE BOOT.

Why did the cowboy shoot a hole
through the book of Genesis?

BECAUSE HE BELIEVED IN THE
BIG BANG THEORY.

Why did the ewe butt the outlaw?

BECAUSE HE WAS ON THE LAM.

**"WHAT'S WITH THIS
'TALLY HO, THE FOX' JAZZ,
WHIPLASH?"**

**"YOU'RE RIGHT,
IT DOESN'T HAPPEN OFTEN."**

"I WOULD HARDLY
CALL IT A STAMPEDE, BRUMLEY."

"WHERE DID YOU LEARN TO MAKE
A COOK-FIRE, COWBOY?"

COWBOY WANNABES

YOU'RE NOT A REAL COWBOY IF YOU:

Think a bucking bronco is a
four-wheel drive
with bad suspension.

Believe mustangs
run best on high octane.

YOU'RE NOT A REAL COWBOY IF YOU:

Wonder how cattle drive
without a license.

Your best
eight-second ride
was on a
roller coaster.

YOU'RE NOT A REAL COWBOY IF YOU:

Believe rodeo
is the name
of a pricey
shopping district
in Beverly Hills.

Think a rodeo
has four wheels
and sits in your driveway.

YOU'RE NOT A REAL COWBOY IF YOU:

Think Louis L'Amour
wore a sarong in old "Road" movies.

Think a bridle path is what
leads the groom to the church.

YOU'RE NOT A REAL COWBOY IF YOU:

Believe a necktie party
is an event to show cowboys
the latest trend in fashion.

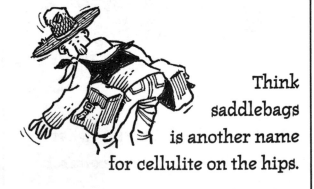

Think
saddlebags
is another name
for cellulite on the hips.

YOU'RE NOT A REAL COWBOY IF YOU:

Think that Smith & Wesson
is a bank.

Hear "Yahoo!"
and look for an Internet link.

YOU'RE NOT A REAL COWBOY IF YOU:

Believe chew is a verb.

Think taking a dip
means going swimming.

YOU'RE NOT A REAL COWBOY IF YOU:

Know eight foreign words
for coffee.

Think grub
refers to being dirty.

YOU'RE NOT A REAL COWBOY IF YOU:

Believe chow is an
expensive dog,
or a trendy way to say good-bye.

Think tanning
your hide
requires
sunscreen
and
artificial lights.

YOU'RE NOT A REAL COWBOY IF YOU:

Believe gas is something
that fuels your truck.

Think pintos
are really ugly cars.

YOU'RE NOT A REAL COWBOY IF YOU:

Believe the Alamo
is where you rent a car.

Consider calf roping a fun game
involving women's legs.

YOU'RE NOT A REAL COWBOY IF YOU:

Think poker
is a good way to get
your wife's attention.

Only wear your boots
on weekends.

YOU'RE NOT A REAL COWBOY IF YOU:

Run to the kitchen
when someone
mentions open range.

Think a
saddle blanket
is used to keep
your saddle warm.

YOU'RE NOT A REAL COWBOY IF YOU:

Believe a nag is someone like
your mother-in-law.

Pick
road apples.

YOU'RE NOT A REAL COWBOY IF YOU:

Believe a stallion
is a swarthy Italian guy.

Think the round bulge
in the rear pocket
of a man's jeans
is a designer label.

YOU'RE NOT A REAL COWBOY IF YOU:

Think
a halter
is a skimpy blouse.

NO ONE DIES

Old cowboys never die;
they just move out of range.

Old Marlboro cowboys
never die;
they just go up in smoke.

Old rattlers
never die;
they just
bite the dust.
Or sometimes
they just strike out.

Old milk cows never die;
they just kick the bucket.

Old beef cattle never die;
they just have too much at steak.

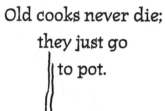

Old cooks never die;
they just go
to pot.

Old broncs never die;
they just lose their kick.

Or sometimes they just
pass the buck.

Old sharpshooters
never die;
they just go out with a bang.

"WATCH OUT FOR
HIS LEFT HOOK, HAYSEED."

"I NEVER SEEN ANYONE
GET BUCKED OFF
WITH SUCH FLAIR."

"I WANT TO MAKE IT PERFECTLY CLEAR
WHO IS BOSS OF THIS OUTFIT."

MORE COWBOY WISDOM

Lightning
never
strikes twice.
It gets the job done
the first time.

A cowboy isn't
narrow-minded;
the world's just too wide.

If cowboys are real men,
how come they wear
high heels?

The difference between
a cowboy and a brother-in-law
is one rides the bull,
and the other shoots it.

Cowboys know that
if you try something
for the first time,
try it alone.

Ain't
no ailment
a cowboy can get
that a good bottle
of whiskey
can't cure.

What do
Madonna and a cowboy
have in common?
They both wear high heels
and leather pants.

Wearing a Stetson
doesn't make you a cowboy
just like standing in a barn
doesn't make you a horse.

If you want
a loyal friend,
get a dog.

If you see a rabbit
and no one's chasing it,
times ain't
too tough.

If the buzzards
ain't circling,
no one's hungry.

The psychologist told the cowboy
that quitting the wide-open spaces
would leave him de-ranged.

If you lead a cowboy
to whiskey,
you won't need
to make him drink.

Horse thieving
ain't nothing
but a wild noose chase.

People who live
in glass houses
should get someone else
to build their privies.

Real cowgirls never give a
diamondback.

A good rope,
like a busy schedule,
can keep a man tied up
for weeks.

A cowboy
who holds his tongue
has few fences
to mend.

Dancing girls
are like rattlesnakes;
when things start shaking,
it's best to leave them alone.

Cowboys are
like steaks;
the tender ones
are rare.

Oh give me a home
where the buffalo roam,
and I'll show you
one place cowboys
won't have to
wipe their feet.

Don't spit
on another man's boots.
He might be a gunfighter.

It's not whether you spin or dip,
it's how you sway the dame.

Don't be a jerk.
The ranch foreman
doesn't like you
doing his job.

Remember when
bulls, colts, cowboys,
mavericks, and rangers
referred to something
other than sports teams?

It's okay to ask your dog
to cook your breakfast,
but never ask your gal
to fetch your slippers.

A cowboy's heart
is as big
as the great outdoors,
and so's his hat.

A cowboy
can take a dip
without getting wet
and chew
without swallowing.

I wear a Stetson;
therefore I am.